Artist: Jeff Ferneng

To see more of Jeff's artwork cl

www.seefernpaint.com

Author: Douglas Esper

Graphic Designer: Theraisa K. Fleig

http://www.theraisak.com - info@theraisak.com

For more information or to interact with **Sammy and his friends**
(with word puzzles, coloring pages, and more)
check out *http://www.sammysfriends.com*
or E-mail: *info@sammysfriends.com*

and be sure to lookout for <u>the next book</u> in the Sammy series!

ISBN: 1-4392-2297-5

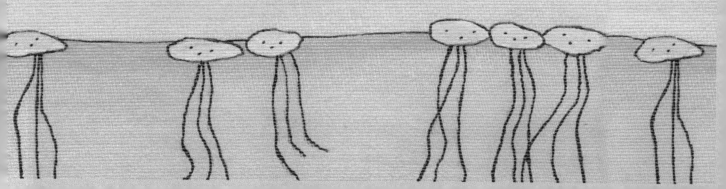

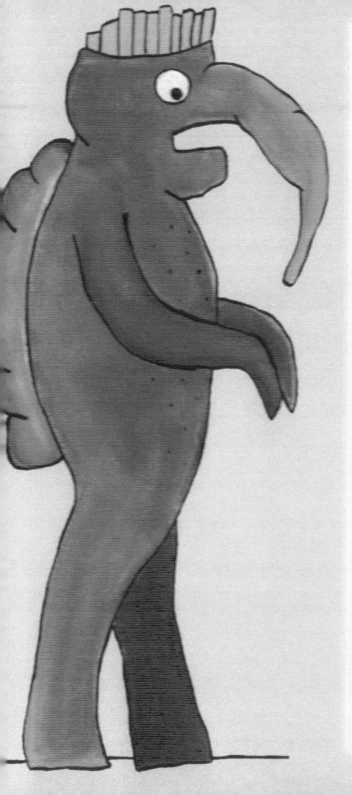

Sammy is PURPLE.

Sammy is Tall

Most importantly,
Sammy is the friendliest
creature of them all.

Sammy likes to *smile*.

Sammy likes to wave.

Sammy lives with his family
in a cozy little cave.

Sammy likes *summer* the best without a doubt.

He loves waking up and then **HURRYING** out.

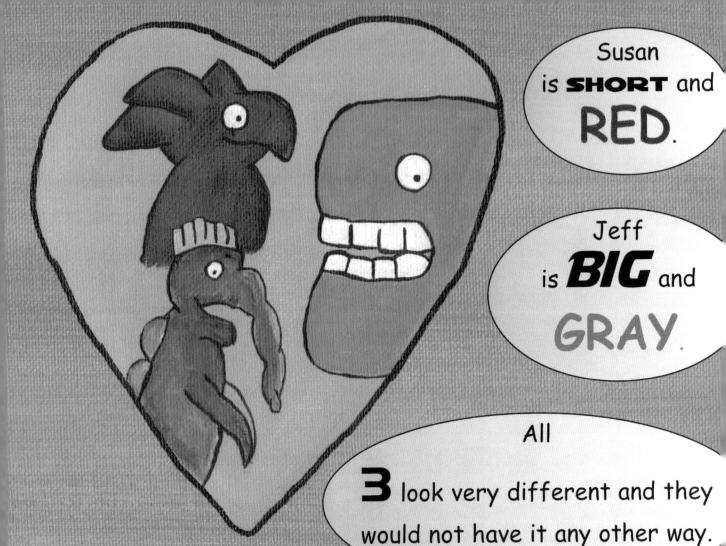

Susan is **SHORT** and RED.

Jeff is **BIG** and GRAY.

All 3 look very different and they would not have it any other way.

"It is what is inside," Sammy's mommy told him before. "Within our hearts is a special place for all the love we store."

Sammy goes to **school.**

It is just over the **_hill._**

Sammy wants to be a doctor and maybe some day he will.

His teacher is fun. Her name is **Miss Hooks.**

Sammy loves it when she reads the class **BOOKS.**

Jeff, Susan and Sammy like to go to the **STORE**.

There they can buy apple slices and carrot sticks galore!

At the store is Mr. Jacobs; he is a friendly man indeed.

He is never too busy to help you find whatever you need.

On Sammy's **BIRTHDAY** he raced to the pond.

With his friends he wanted to play. He was so excited to see his friends on his **special day**.

Sammy waited and waited, but his friends did not show.

"Did they forget my birthday?" Sammy wanted to know.

So...

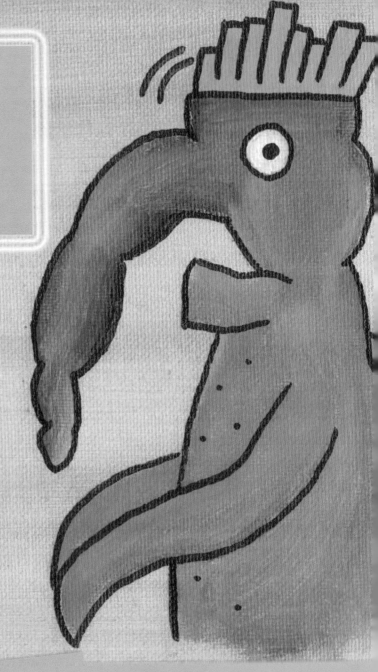

Sammy looked to the **_left._**

Sammy did not see his friends.

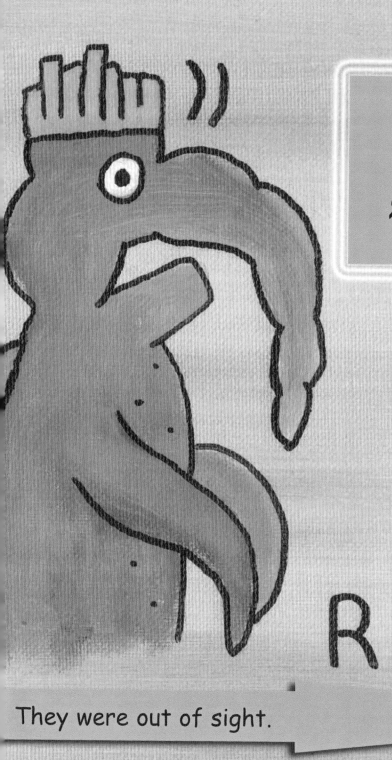

Sammy looked to the **right.**

R

They were out of sight.

With no **super fast** Susan or jumping high Jeff. His birthday would not be fUn and so Sammy left.

Sammy vowed to find his **friends** - he would search all day. He would find them and then go to the pond to *play*.

He looked at Jeff's home; but they were not to be found. Sammy *listened* for them, but did not hear a sound.

He *knocked* on their door hoping to ask Jeff's parents. But no one was home maybe they had to *run* errands.

He looked at the school, but all the lights were out.

"Where can they be?" Sammy said from his snout.

There were no bright yellow buses or any blue minivans.

No crossing guard, no laughing kids, no practicing marching bands.

Sammy walked to the store hoping to find his friends. But on the door was a sign, which now Sammy read:

"The store is closed today for a special occasion."

Sammy thought perhaps Mr. Jacobs had left on vacation.

Now Sammy was determined to search the whole town.

He called...

JEFF!

And he called...

SUSAN!

Hoping they would hear the sound.

Sammy returned to the pond, but alas he could see. He said, "Jeff and Susan are not here to play with me."

Sammy started to **Cry.** He was sad and alone.

He started to walk slowly towards his cozy little home.

He got to the door and said,

"My birthday was no fun. I did not play, I did not sing, and I did not even run. I did not see Jeff jumping or Susan running a race, I received no presents, birthday cards,

or even a birthday cake!"

But then Sammy opened the door...

His cave was full of family, friends, and folks from all over town.

They shouted

"HAPPY BIRTHDAY!"

all at once, and it was the loudest sound!

Sammy was so happy and he was so full of **joy**, but it was not because of the *cake* he ate or even his brand new toys.

Sammy was smiling because he had searched high and low.

He had searched up the hilltops down to the valleys below.

He had gone to **houses**, the *school*, and even to the store.

Sammy had searched *everywhere* until he could search no more.

But just when he had **lost** all hope and thought his *search* would never end,

Sammy had come home, and at
LAST...

Sammy had found his
SPECIAL friends!

COLOR SAMMY BY NUMBER

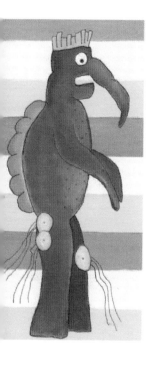

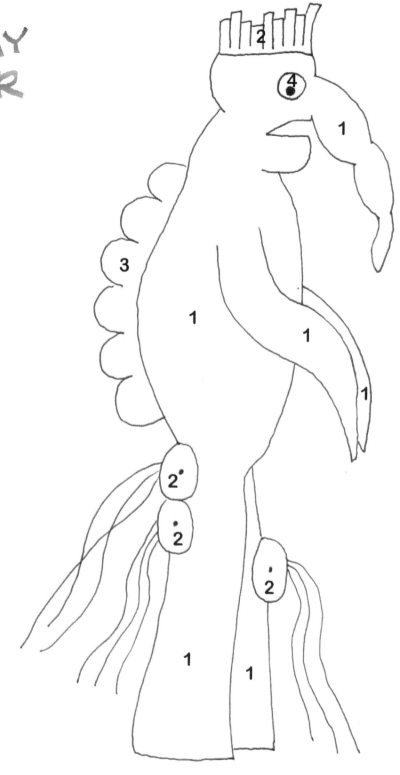

1	**Purple**
2	**Pink**
3	**Blue**
4	**White**